Samantha Berger
Daniel Moreton

Scholastic Inc.
New York • Toronto • London • Auckland • Sydney

Acknowledgments

Literacy Specialist: Linda Cornwell

Social Studies Consultant: Barbara Schubert, Ph.D.

Design: Silver Editions

Photo Research: Silver Editions

Endnotes: Jacqueline Smith

Endnote Illustrations: Anthony Carnabucia

Photographs: Cover: Frank Siteman/Tony Stone Images; p.1: D. Young-Wolff/Photo Edit; p. 2: Jon Riley/Tony Stone Images; p. 3: F. Pedrick/The Image Works; p. 4: Bill Aron/Photo Edit; p. 5: Myrleen Cate/Tony Stone Images; p. 6: Jose Carrillo/Stock Boston; p. 7: Bob Daemmrich/The Image Works; p. 8: Terry Vine/Tony Stone Images; p. 9: Frank Siteman/Tony Stone Images; p.10: Susan Baker; p. 11: Rita Nanni/Photo Researchers, Inc.; p. 12: Bill Bachmann/Photo Edit.

Library of Congress Cataloging-in-Publication Data
Berger, Samantha.
Celebrations / Samantha Berger, Daniel Moreton.
p. cm. -- (Social studies emergent readers)
Summary: Simple text and photographs explore various occasions
for celebrations, including birthdays, weddings, and giving thanks.
ISBN 0-439-04557-6 (pbk.: alk. paper)
1. Holidays--Juvenile literature. 2. Special days--Juvenile literature.
[1. Special days.] I. Moreton, Daniel. II. Title. III. Series.
GT3933.B47 1999

394.26--dc21

98-50496
CIP AC

2   3   4   5   6   7   8   9   10   08   03   02   01   00   99

Celebrations.

Celebrations for our birthdays.

Happy birthday!

Celebrations for special people.

I love you, Mom!

Celebrations for giving thanks.

Thank you!

Celebrations for playing a game.

Nice game!

Celebrations for getting married.

Congratulations!

Celebrations for being together.

Celebrations

Whether it's a holiday, a birthday, an important achievement, or a special family event, many families get together and celebrate. There might be food, dance, song, cards, gifts, or presents, but there are always smiles when we celebrate!

Happy Birthday! In the U.S. and many other countries, children's birthdays are celebrated with a birthday cake with candles, presents, cards, games, and singing. The "Happy Birthday" song, written by an American kindergarten teacher 100 years ago, is now sung in many different languages around the world. Some countries have very different birthday traditions. In China, everyone eats noodles to wish the birthday child a long life. In Mexico, children are blindfolded and strike a piñata until it breaks and all the goodies spill out. In Ireland, the birthday child is turned upside-down and bumped on the floor, one bump for each year of life plus one for good luck.

I love you, Mom! On Mother's Day we show how much we love and appreciate our mothers with cards, presents, or just by doing something nice together. The first Mother's Day celebrations were thousands of years ago, in ancient Greece, where they celebrated Rhea, the mother of the gods. An American woman named Anna Jarvis helped to make Mother's Day an official holiday in the U.S. Now it is celebrated in many countries, though not on the same day.

Thank you! At Thanksgiving we get together with our relatives to appreciate each other and everything we have. Many people celebrate with a huge dinner of turkey, pumpkin pie, cranberry sauce, and other dishes. The tradition started with a feast the first settlers held in 1621 to give thanks for the harvest and for surviving their first difficult year in America. Many other cultures have festivals to give thanks for the harvest, for health, or for life.

Nice game! Winning a game is an exciting achievement. We celebrate athletic successes with trophies, parties, and team songs. Sometimes several people pick up one of the winners and carry that person around on their shoulders.

Best wishes! Weddings are joyful celebrations of love. In almost all wedding celebrations there are music, dancing, flowers, presents, special wedding clothes, speeches, food, and the good wishes of friends. There are many interesting wedding traditions from around the world. At a Chinese wedding, the bride wears red, not white. At a Jewish wedding, the groom must step on and break a glass to symbolize that he will have the strength to get the couple through life's problems. At an Italian wedding, each guest receives hard candy-covered almonds in beautiful boxes.

Sometimes, even a day at the beach or a walk in the park can be a celebration—a celebration of being together as a family.